SPIRITUALLY

LIMPING

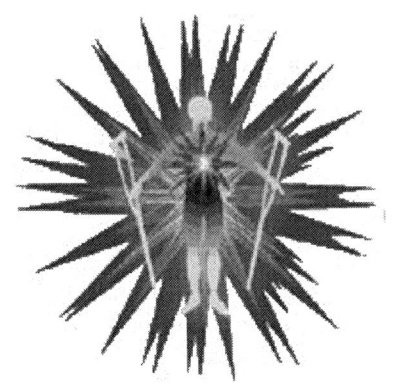

I MAY BE LIMPING

BUT I AM STILL WALKING

Elder Elaine R. Westbrook

Spiritually Limping

I May Be Limping But I Am Still Walking

Second Edition

Copyright 2003 - Elaine R. Westbrook

Memphis, TN

All rights reserved. No portion of this book may be reproduced in any form, except for brief quotations in reviews, without the written permission of the author.

Published By:
E's Graphics
Manuscript Edited by:
Minister Kimbria N. Westbrook, Memphis, TN
Mr. Law Wilcher, Sr., Memphis, TN

ISBN 1-59196-382-6

Resources:

King James Version of The Holy Bible
Unless otherwise indicated

MORRIS' COMMENTARY
Stanley L. Morris Th.D.
Morris' Introductions to the Books of the Bible

MATTHEW HENRY
Concise Commentary on the Whole Bible by Matthew Henry

CHARLES SWINDOLL
Perfect Trust

Additional copies of this book may be obtained via
www.ewestbooks.com

Dedication

*The book is dedicated to My Father, My Saviour and My Comforter...**The Holy Trinity**. I would also like to dedicate this writing to all those whom the Lord has allowed to touch my life, my earthly father, the late Mr. Hugh Roberson, my mother; Mrs. Emily Roberson, my siblings, children, friends, acquaintances, and especially my spiritual mentors. There are those who were only there for a season, some only for a reason, but especially those who are with me for a lifetime.*

I would especially like to thank my editors, Minister Kimbria Westbrook (my one daughter, whom I love dearly and am so proud of) and Mr. Law Wilcher, Sr. (a good friend in the time of need). Without the two of you the readers would have had many unanswered questions, typos and several run-on sentences. I love and thank you both.

Introduction

The Lord inspired me to write a book on this very subject... "Spiritually Limping". It is my firm belief that many of us in church professing to be Christians are limping, which simply means that we are facing or have faced some struggles in their personal walk with God. While it may not something that we like to talk about, our struggles have a purpose. There are some struggles that are ordained by God Himself, to serve as testimonies. Our struggles become or can our testimonies, which can help others along the way. It is however tragic that during our struggles we discover that for most people in church they cannot always speak out about their limping... for some reason we have forgotten that the church is a hospital to the sick.

It is in church that we should find our healing instead we find criticisms, put-downs, and unforgiving saints. Jacob wrestled with God, but I believe that in fact his wrestling was more with who he was, his past and all of his mistakes. When God touched him he was then changed! Yes, he was left with a limp but I believe that was his outward sign of his encounter with God. In our imperfections God can be glorified. Jacob limped after the struggle was over, but his life was indeed changed for the better. To those looking on they saw a physical limp, the inward limping that could not

so easily be seen was far worse. If we could ask Jacob I am sure he would not trade the outward limping for the inward limping any day.

This book was written to help those of us in the church who are struggling with a specific area in our lives... one that causes us to walk this Christian walk with a limp. It is not designed to give us an excuse or to cause us to glory in our limping. It is however, written to help us get real with ourselves, our Christian brothers and sisters, and most importantly with God. The Lord, who is omniscient, knew us before we were ever formed in our mother's womb, and yet He called us to be His disciples. He knows everything that we have done and will ever do and yet He loves us and chooses to use us anyway. God knows who we really are.

What we accomplish in the work of the Kingdom is not a credit to us, or anything that we could do in our own might. Kingdom work is not our work but God's work; we are only vessels that He has chosen to carry out His divine plan for mankind.

KJV Jeremiah 1:5-8

5. *Before I formed thee in the belly I knew thee; and before thou camest forth out of the womb I sanctified thee, and I ordained thee a prophet unto the nations.*

6. *Then said I, Ah, Lord God! behold, I cannot speak: for I am a child.*

7. *But the Lord said unto me, Say not, I am a child: for thou shalt go to all that I shall send thee, and whatsoever I command thee thou shalt speak.*

8. *Be not afraid of their faces: for I am with thee to deliver thee, saith the Lord.*

When we find our walk being hindered by a limp, let us be real concerning our weakness and continue on, fasting and praying, until the Lord either delivers us or strengthens us for the journey, then give God the glory for His mighty works. Let us no longer make excuses, hide out or concern ourselves with what others may think or say, for the Lord God shall be with us. Say not that I am limping, instead ***Keep On Walking!*** **When we confess our sin… the Word says that God is faithful and just to forgive us.**

Foreword

With all that is happening in the world today – especially in Christendom, Elder Elaine Westbrook's **Spiritually Limping** is a timely, in season work that is sure to be a blessing to those who have become victims of their own decisions and circumstances. The one thing that we must always remember is that the Lord allows nothing to occur in the life of the believer to destroy us, but it is designed to discipline us and bring our commitments into proper focus. That's why we will find ourselves constantly being challenged and stretched; that's why many of us will find ourselves, if we're not there already, at an uncomfortable place in our walk with God. What we have to do is look at all of life's circumstances through the eyes of God and only then will we be able to agree with the Apostle Paul when he says, *"Therefore I take pleasure in infirmities, in reproaches, in necessities, in persecutions, in distresses for Christ's sake: for when I am weak, then am I strong"*.

Many times, our deliverances will come in a form that is unusual and strange to us. God did not promise that our deliverance would involve the removal of a circumstance or condition, but He did promise that His grace would be sufficient. Through our *limping,* God teaches us one of the great mysteries of the faith. When God gets ready to give us more of Him, He has to make sure that more of Him will not be too much for us. Many will suggest that *limping* is merely to humble us; I conclude that God has a greater purpose in mind. The ultimate goal of God is to allow us to experience – first hand – the sufficiency of His grace. Paul said it himself in Romans 5:20 when he said, *"Where sin did abound, grace did much more abound"*. Grace does not become a reality for us until we have something in our life that requires the grace of God to cover. The greater my *limp*, the more dependent I am on the grace of God.

> The greater your struggle with yourself, the greater your dependence on the sufficiency of God's grace.

Elder Westbrook's **Spiritually Limping** gives us a fresh look at what it truly means to struggle and yet remain anointed. Our *limp* is there for a reason – it's there to mold your character, to chisel you into the man or woman God has called you to be, to show you that you can't have a problem that God can't touch.

Overseer W. James Thomas, II, D.D.

Senior Pastor, Shiloh Church of Memphis

Memphis, Tennessee

Excerpts

"The church today has been trying to imitate and adapt to the world instead of setting the example for the world. This has caused us to tolerate things in the church and in us that have no connection to God.

Our walk, therefore, has been tainted by our trying to carry around the things of this world instead of the things of God. We are the light that should be shining brightly, but instead the overshadowing of the world's devises has dimmed us."

"As an unsaved person we are much like the caterpillar, crawling around leaving a trail of slime behind us as we consume and devour whatever we desire. We have no protective covering which makes it easy for us to be destroyed. We are destructive and unattractive and we take on many forms and have many names."

"Will the Lord continue to grow our churches, save the lost through us, or use us to reach the unsaved when we

ourselves are not what we profess to be? Our membership may grow, but not with the unsaved, instead only with more hurting and limping saints. The church today is limping… our walk is awkward, irregular, lame and unsteady."

Table of Contents

Chapter 1	Page 1
Limping Defined	
Chapter 2	Page 11
Living Beneath The Promises of God	
Chapter 3	Page 16
The Faith To Walk This Walk	
Chapter 4	Page 33
Jacob's Limp	
Chapter 5	Page 42
Saved, But Limping	
Chapter 6	Page 52
The Problem Is With Us	
Chapter 7	Page 67
Restoration	

Chapter One

Limping Defined

As Christians how many of us are walking this walk of Christendom with a limp? The word "limping" implies that while you are indeed walking, your walk is *lame, unsteady, halting, and with irregularity.* Your walk *is irregular, jerky and/or awkward.* To walk with a limp indicates that there is something wrong with either one side of you or the other.

LIMPING is defined as:
intr.v. **limped, limp·ing, limps**

1. To walk lamely, especially with irregularity, as if favoring one leg.

2. To move or proceed haltingly or unsteadily: *The project limped along with half it's previous funding.*

n. An irregular, jerky, or awkward gait.

Spiritually Limping

- **Limping**

Limp \Limp\ (l[i^]mp), v. i. [imp. & p. p. Limped (l[i^]mt; 215); p. pr. & vb. n. Limping.] [Cf. AS. lemphealt lame, OHG. limphen to limp, be weak; perh. akin to E. lame, or to limp, a [root]120.] To halt; to walk lamely.

The writer of the book of James records that "a double-minded man is unstable in all his ways". *(KJV James 1:8)* This could account for a person's walk being irregular, jerky, or awkward. It would definitely lend itself to a person's walk being irregular.

An injury to your leg or foot would cause you to walk with a limp. Should your body become afflicted with something such as arthritis, rheumatism, or another one of the crippling diseases that affects your joints… you will walk with a limp. Likewise in the Spirit, should you become a victim of the disease of sin, you will also walk with a limp.

Sin is the one thing that we are all susceptible to. Whether it is the sin of fornication, adultery, drinking, gambling, lying, cheating, stealing, unfaithfulness, boasting, arrogance, laziness, backbiting, unbelief, incest, envy, jealousy, deceit, blasphemy, homosexuality, lesbianism, sexual perversion, or anything else that is unrighteous…*"for all unrighteousness is sin." (KJV 1 John 5:17)* Sin is the main thing that could definitely cause a Christian to walk with a limp.

My limp can be caused by the weight of that thing that I am struggling with. It has begun to weigh me down to the point that my walking is unbalanced. Up to a point, I am able to cover up my limp and pretend that there is not a problem in my walk. Over time; however, that thing begins to cause so much of a disturbance in my spirit that I cannot hide it anymore. That is the problem with carrying around a weight that does not line up with what is natural for me to be carrying. I am not designed to carry around sin.

Do not misunderstand; while walking with a limp is not where any of us would like to find ourselves, the good thing is that we are yet walking. The most important thing is that we continue to walk with God. Our limp may slow us down or cause others to stare at us and wonder if we will make the journey, but it does not have to completely stop us. There may not be any pride in walking with a limp, but praise God you are still walking. You may not get there first; however, the race is not given to the swift, but to the one that endureth to the end... *keep on walking*. There are too many people who have given up or will give up on their walk with the Lord because they cannot seem to get over their limping, or that which caused them to limp.

What does it mean to walk with a limp, in this our Christian walk? To walk with a limp means simply that something is wrong with me. The question is this, is my limp a result of something I have done or something I am doing? If so, that can be fixed. However, if my limping is a result of what God is allowing me to endure so that I will come out with a testimony, all I can do is endure as a good soldier and keep on walking. I might have to limp in front of all of the deacons, choir members or the preachers. The whole church might have to see me limp, but only God and I know the real reason behind my limp.

Yes, I walk with a limp, but I am still walking. My limp may come from alcohol or drugs but if I keep on walking, one day I can walk right out of the situation that is causing me to limp. I can gain strength, be delivered, and walk upright before God because I kept on walking. My deliverance is in my continuing to walk, so I cannot give up. I have got to keep on walking, limp or no limp. I must keep on walking.

Many people may criticize me because of my limp. They may talk about me because of this limp in my walk. The whole congregation may know of my problem and try to cast me aside because I am walking with a limp. But, if I endure the hard times as a good soldier and continue to limp my way into the presence of God, I will one day be delivered and my walk will be upright. At that point, my endurance and continual walk will become a testimony to others that God's power can and will keep us and deliver us out of all our sin… if we only stay in the race.

David walked with a limp, and is now remembered as one of the greatest men in the Bible. David, who was anointed to be king when he was only a boy tending his father's sheep, walked with a limp. David, who while being chased by Saul and was divinely protected by the Lord, had a problem. David, the man after God's own heart, had a limp in his walk. David lusted after another mans wife, committed adultery and had her husband killed to cover his sin. David walked with a limp. Yes, he was a great warrior, the anointed king, a writer of the largest amount of the Psalms, a man that loved the Lord, but he walked with a limp.

While we cannot condone the sins of David we have to take note that the one thing he never did, was to lose sight of whom he served. Even in his sin, David sought the Lord. In other words, David kept on walking. Yes, he had a limp, but he kept on walking. You must be so committed to God that regardless of your limping, you will still continue this walk.

KJV Psalms 51:9-12

9) Hide thy face from my sins, and blot out all mine iniquities.
10) Create in me a clean heart, O God; and renew a right spirit within me.
11) Cast me not away from thy presence; and take not thy Holy Spirit from me.
12) Restore unto me the joy of thy salvation; and uphold me with thy free spirit.

The Bible sets before us examples for every situation that we might find ourselves in today. For this reason, it is the living and abiding Word of God. It is as applicable today as it was when it was first written. I believe that the Holy Spirit allowed us to know of David's sin, his shortcomings, his prayers, his restoration and his relationship with God in order to show us that we too can fall short but yet be loved, protected, and used by God.

Spiritually Limping

There are many of us walking today with a limp, but like David we are yet walking.

You have got to say, my walk might be awkward, jerky, or irregular but I must keep on walking. It is only when I continue to walk that the Lord will deliver me. It is only when I keep going on that I can gain enough faith to trust fully in the Lord and receive my healing. I might have to limp for a while, I might have to limp in front of my family and friends and I might have to limp on my way to church, but, if I have to limp all the way, I am going to be found walking, because the Lord, Himself, is with me ALWAYS!

Rev. Robert E. Slater put it this way. *"Sometimes in our journeying with God we find we are spiritually limping. Our prayer life dries up. Our fear trumps our faith; our guilt exceeds our joy. We limp along in the spiritual journey when we don't put all our weight on God's grace."*

---

[1] Rev. Robert E. Slater, First Presbyterian Church Port Townsend, WA. Sermon entitled "Journeying with God when Limping".

Spiritually Limping

When I am seen limping, it proves that I am attempting to walk. I could hide my limp by deciding to just stop walking, that way no one would have to know that I have a limp. If I just stayed at home and decided not to go to the church, I could hide the fact that I have a limp. I could try to handle this situation all on my own and pretend just for a little while that I am walking upright and maybe I would not be found out. But in my flesh I am only able to handle this situation temporarily…I need the Lord to deliver me, then my deliverance would be complete and lasting.

One of the problems with us as believers is that we are so caught up in what other people think, that we try to hide our shortcomings, thereby failing to seek the help that we have been promised, thus failing to receive our deliverance. There is no shame in having a problem the shame is in not getting help for the problem. We all need help in one way or another and sometimes it is in the fellowship of other believers that we can seek the Lord's help and corporately take our problems to Him. Some of us limp as an example of what God can do. When the disciples asked Jesus *"who sinned this man or his* parents", his answer was *"no one, but this was in order that the glory of the Lord could be revealed"*.

KJV John 9:2-3
And his disciples asked him, saying, Master, who did sin, this man, or his parents, that he was born blind?
Jesus answered, neither hath this man sinned, nor his parents: but that the works of God should be made manifest in him.

Yet, in some cases, our limp is due to our own choices and sin, but when we give even this to the Lord, He gets the glory out of our deliverance.

Chapter Two

Living Beneath The Promises of God

Another word used by Webster's dictionary to describe limping is *"to be weak"*. Is it not our weaknesses that can ultimately lead us into sin? In other words, when we are weak to something and give in to that weakness, our walk can be hindered, thus causing us to limp. Regardless to what your particular weakness is, when you give in to it, you begin to walk with a limp.

The Scriptures tell us to *"cast all of our burdens on the Lord"*.

KJV Psalms 55:22
Cast thy burden upon the Lord, and he shall sustain thee: he shall never suffer the righteous to be moved.

When we are weak He is strong and His grace is sufficient.

The things that cause us to limp are those things that we try in our limited humanity, to handle. The Lord has declared in His Word that He would bear our infirmities. Our charge is to bring them all to Him.

As a child of God we are not expected to fight our own battles. Yes, we are instructed to go to the fight, but when we enter the battlefield our enemies are already defeated by the power of **His** might. *"This battle is not yours, it belongs to the Lord".* (2 Chronicles 20:15) The words echo throughout our spirits as we recite them and even sing them, but in truth we are often times defeated because we try to fight the battle ourselves. *"Greater is He that is in you than he that is in the world" (1 John 4:4).*

Understanding that our battles are not physical battles, but instead, spiritual fights that therefore must be fought in the spirit realm. When we fail to turn over all of our problems

Spiritually Limping

To the Lord, we are taking the first step to defeat. The Bible tells us that we are more than conquerors through Him that loves us. (Romans 8:37) When we take a closer look at this passage the first thing that should stand out is the word *"we"*. Who then is the *"we"* of this passage? We, are the chosen ones, the called out ones, the set aside ones. Much of the church consists of the saints of God, the sanctified ones... the believers. As believers we have the promise of God that we are not just conquerors, but *"more than conquerors"*. Conquerors overcome odds that are possible for either side or team to beat. Being more than a conqueror means conquering odds that would otherwise be impossible to beat.

Beating the odds against cancer in its final stages is being more than a conqueror. Returning to the doctor's office and them finding no more traces of HIV in your blood is being more than a conqueror. Living years after the doctors pronounce little to no chance of recovery or death on you is being more than a conqueror. When you stop smoking, drinking, using drugs, prostituting, gambling or living a homosexual lifestyle without the aid of support groups or medical treatments that is being more than a conqueror. A single mother on a limited income, rearing children to become Godly, honest, hardworking, income producing citizens is more than a conqueror.

"In all your ways acknowledge him and he will direct your path". (Proverbs 3:6) This is a Scripture that offers us an alternative to walking with a limp. In everything that we do, we are called to acknowledge or to recognize Him. When we truly recognize God as our unlimited provider, healer, deliverer, creator and Saviour in everything that we encounter, we have taken the first step to walking upright.
One of the biggest problems with today's believer is the failure to see who God really is. Perhaps this is why we are attempting to bring God down to our level, instead of stretching out to reach up to His level. In the days of Moses, Israel saw great and astounding miracles, impossible for man to recreate or explain. This, undoubtedly, added to their knowledge of God and His awesome power.

Throughout the Bible, people came face to face with the power of God, power that was otherwise unexplainable. Today, our faith suffers partly due to the knowledge that mankind has acquired. Science attempts to explain away the Biblical account of creation, as well as many of the miracles described in the Bible. We have in part fallen victim to some of the false teachings that attempt to explain what the Bible calls miracles.

Chapter Three

The Faith To Walk This Walk

"Faith is supposedly a crutch, but that's what so many of us need because we are limping, at least spiritually and emotionally."
Bishop F. Josephus Johnson
Akron's House of the Lord

NIV Hebrews 11:1
Now faith is being sure of what we hope for and certain of what we do not see.
NIV 2 Corinthians 5:7
We live by faith, not by sight.
KJV 2 Corinthians 5:7
(For we walk by faith, not by sight:)

Our walking with a limp or walking upright is a direct result of our faith in God. The writer of the book of Hebrews says… *"Now, faith is…."*. Our faith in God and who He is, cannot afford to be shaken to the point that we the believers fail to walk in that faith. It is our faith, and our faith, alone that cause us to believe regardless to the teachings, explanations or scientific reproductions or accomplishments that would try to make us doubt God. It is our faith that can move God to the point of action. When we believe in the face of all opposition and we stand on that belief, God is stirred into honoring that faith even if it means going against the laws of nature. Creative miracles are seen when faith stands boldly against all the opposition, doctor's reports, test results or man's attempts to prove his superiority over God.

It may be that those of us, who are limping, fail to see more of God's creative miracles today because our faith is so weak. What some of us have is what I call, *a speaking faith.* We declare boldly that we believe that God is a healer, but when faced with a bad doctor's report we cave in to the fear of death and the unknown. It has become so easy for us to speak one thing while our life portrays another. When faced with death, how many of us can stand boldly and declare our unwavering faith in God? Can we till have faith when the doctor says there is no hope, or when we see our loved ones appear to be slipping away?

When death comes, and our young ones are gone, can we stand strong and say as Job did, *"the Lord giveth and the Lord taketh away, blessed be the name of the Lord"*. How many pastors have heard the question, *"Why did God allow this or that to happen"?*

Most Christians have become so adaptive to their surroundings that adjustments have become easy. We adapt to the world even though we are supposed to be the ones that set the standards for the rest of the world. Instead of conforming to the world's standards and imitating them, the Apostle Paul wrote in Romans 12:1-2 that we are called to be transformed from it, by the renewing of our minds. We in the Christian world should be setting standards instead of following them. The Bible says that we are to be the head and not the tail. The head leads and the tail follows.

KJV Deuteronomy 28:13

And the Lord shall make thee the head, and not the tail; and thou shalt be above only, and thou shalt not be beneath; if that thou hearken unto the commandments of The Lord thy God, which I command thee this day, to observe and to do them:

We are said to be *"the salt"* in this world, meaning that we are supposed to be the flavor in this world. Instead we are being flavored by the world.

KJV Matthew 5:13-14.

13. Ye are the salt of the earth: but if the salt have lost his savour, wherewith shall it be salted? It is thenceforth good for nothing, but to be cast out, and to be trodden under foot of men.
14. Ye are the light of the world. A city that is set on a hill cannot be hid.

The church today has been trying to imitate and adapt to the world instead of setting the example for the world. This has caused us to tolerate things in the church and in us that have no connection to God. Our walk, therefore, has been tainted by our trying to carry around the things of this world instead of the things of God. We are the light that should be shining brightly, but instead the overshadowing of the world's devises has dimmed us.

We are limping around, weak, and without the power that has been promised to us. Our ministries are struggling because there is not enough power being displayed that our light shines brightly enough for the sinner to find his way to Christ. They are being hindered by our limp and not being lead by our walk. If we are ever going to reach the lost and save the world for Christ we must begin to understand and accept God's plan for our lives and His Church. This is the only way we will be able to live and be seen as living epistles.

KJV Romans 12:1-2

I beseech you therefore, brethren, by the mercies of God, that ye present your bodies a living sacrifice, holy, acceptable unto God, which is your reasonable service. And be not conformed to this world: but be ye transformed by the renewing of your mind, that ye may prove what is that good, and acceptable, and perfect, will of God.

Matthew Henry expounds on this passage by sayings, "*Conversion and sanctification are the renewing of the mind; a change, not of the substance, but of the qualities of the soul. The progress of sanctification, dying to sin more and more, and living to righteousness more and more, is the carrying on this renewing work, till it is perfected in glory.* **The great enemy to this renewal is conformity to this world**. *Take heed of forming plans for happiness, as though it lay in the things of this world, which soon pass away.* **Do not fall in with the customs of those that walk in the lusts of the flesh, and mind earthly things.** *The work of the Holy Ghost first begins in the understanding, and is carried on to the will, affections, and conversation, till there is a change of the whole man into the likeness of*

God, in knowledge, righteousness, and true holiness. Thus, to be godly, is to give up ourselves to God."

Let's look a little closer at one word in this passage…
"Transform"
Strong's Ref. # 3339. Romanized metamorphoo
Pronounced met-am-or-fo'-o; meaning to transform (literally or figuratively, "metamorphose"): KJV--change, transfigure, transform.

Webster's Unabridged Dictionary defines it this way:
• \Trans*form"\, v. t. [imp. & p. p. <u>Transformed</u>; p. pr. & vb. n. <u>Transforming.</u>] [L. transformare, transformatum; trans across, over + formare to from: cf. F. transformer. See <u>Form</u>, v. t.] 1. To change the form of; to change in shape or appearance; to metamorphose; as, a caterpillar is ultimately transformed into a butterfly. Love may transform me to an oyster. --Shak. 2. To change into another substance; to transmute; as, the alchemists sought to transform lead into gold. <u>3. To change in nature, disposition, heart, character, or the like; to convert.</u> Be ye transformed by the renewing of your mind. --Rom. xii. 2.

The Apostle Paul is saying to us that after we have had an encounter with Christ, such as he himself had, on the

Damascus Road, that there should be such a transformation that takes place in our lives, that is so powerful that our very form or appearance is changed, just as the caterpillar is literally transformed into a butterfly. Our experience with the risen Saviour should cause us to be so changed inwardly that our, even our, outward appearance is changed. The older saints used to say something like, *"There is something on the inside working on the outside that has made a change in my life"*.

Notice the caterpillar, there is nothing attractive about it. It crawls instead of walks; it leaves film behind it everywhere it goes. It is so fleshy that it literally is unprotected and easily destroyed. The caterpillar is also known as a worm, it feeds on the leaves and plants and destroys or consumes that which it has not planted.

Easton's Bible Dictionary describes the caterpillar as: "the consumer". Used in the Old Testament (1 Kings 8:37; 2 Chr. 6:28; Ps. 78:46;Isa. 33:4) as the translation of a word (hasil) the root of which means "to devour" or "consume," and which is used also with reference to the

Spiritually Limping

locust in Deut. 8:38. It may have been a species of locust, or the name of one of the transformations through which the locust passes, locust-grub. It is also found (Ps. 105:34; Jer. 51:14, 27; R.V., "cankerworm") as the rendering of a different Hebrew word, _yelek_, a word elsewhere endered "cankerworm" (q.v.), Joel 1:4; 2:25. (See <u>LOCUST</u>.)

As an unsaved person we are much like the caterpillar, crawling around leaving a trail of slime behind us as we consume and devour whatever we desire. We have no protective covering which makes it easy for us to be destroyed. We are destructive and unattractive and we take on many forms and have many names.

A word history reveals that the caterpillar, in one dialect is known also as *"devil's cat"*.

- **Word History:** Larvae of moths and butterflies are popularly seen as resembling other, larger animals. Consider the Italian dialect word *gatta*, "cat, caterpillar" the German dialect term *t?atz*, "caterpillar" (literally "devil's cat"); the French word *chenille*, "caterpillar" (from a Vulgar Latin diminutive, *cancula,* of *canis,* "dog"); and last but not least, our own word *caterpillar,* which appears probably to have come from an unattested Old North French word *catepelose,* meaning literally *"hairy cat."*

We are all born in sin, shaped in iniquity... the seed of Adam. It is only after accepting Jesus, the last Adam, that our sins are forgiven and we no longer belong to this world. Once we are saved or converted, we then have the power to work our way out of our cocoons of sin, taking on the shape of something beautiful with wings that enable us to soar. The only goal in the life of the adult butterfly is to reproduce. As Christians we share the same goal... to reproduce. The Great Commission given to us as believers is also that we should reproduce believers.

KJV Matthew 28:18-20

"And Jesus came and spake unto them, saying, All power is given unto me in heaven and in earth. Go ye therefore, and teach all nations, baptizing them in the name of the Father, and of the Son, and of the Holy Ghost: Teaching them to observe all things whatsoever I have commanded

you: and, lo, I am with you always, even unto the end of the world. Amen."

With such a directive given to us as followers of Jesus Christ, why then are we so fearful of accepting this call to service? What is it about us that cause us to shrink from our duty and return back to what we have been delivered out of? Charles Swindoll wrote, *"It's the nature of the beast within us to keep going back to the familiar rather than to strap on faith and face the future. We are intimated by the adventure, the excitement, and the delight of watching God block out the "giants" in the land."*

He goes on to write, *"Walking with God is the most exciting and rewarding of all experiences on earth. It is also the most difficult… Faith is like lighting the torch that passes from one person to the next. You can't light the torch of another if yours is not burning."*

When we are struggling in the area of faith, God will often times give us others to help build up our faith. In 1 Kings 17, the widow's faith was so weak that she had literally given up. Then came Elijah with a word of promise. The woman could have decided not to listen or believe, but because she did believe and obey, she not only received the promise, but also is assured that her faith had to increase. The faith of Daniel and the faith of the three Hebrew boys, as written of in Daniel chapter 3, had to ignite faith in even those who knew not the God they served.

One of the purposes of the fellowshipping of the saints is to encourage each other, rather than to tear each other down. There is so much conflict and confusion in our churches today that faith building is suffering greatly. Many of our churches can be found engaging in courtroom battles, legal struggles and even violence against one another. Many of the struggles within the members of the congregation often times take a back seat to the power struggles being waged.

Why should the sinner seek our God, or believe in all the spouting that we do, when they can see the bitterness, the anger and warring among those of us called Christians?

Spiritually Limping

Many of those weaker saints are limping around on their weak faith, struggling to make it out to the house of God, only to be met with political battles between pastors and deacons.

If our faith is so weak that we need a judge in a courtroom or the television camera to regulate how church is conducted, then how can we help build up our brother's faith? It certainly cannot help but most assuredly it will serve to tear it down. More importantly, what happens to the evangelistic ministry of the church? It will either be non-existent or have no power to witness to the unsaved. Will our testimony about the goodness, love and mercy of Jesus be heard over our bickering? Satan will be sure to magnify the sounds of the bickering over any testimonies of the goodness of God, which would surely hinder our effectiveness.

Will the Lord continue to grow our churches, save the lost through us, or use us to reach the unsaved when we ourselves are not what we profess to be? Our membership may grow, but not with the unsaved, instead only with more hurting and limping saints. The church today is limping… our walk is *awkward, irregular, lame and unsteady.*

The Bible says that we are called to be *"living epistles",* but how can we be, when we are so uncomfortable being an example of Jesus Christ? To limp is one thing but to be as a millstone around the neck of our brother is another. Our struggles can cause our brothers to stumble. It is vitally important that we not mistake a temporary limp for a more permanent condition. Some of us are at the altar over and over again for the same thing, constantly before the church asking for prayer but never receiving deliverance. But, this is the same principal as going to the bank to make a withdrawal without ever having made a deposit.

You cannot receive what you are asking for. Deliverance comes through a relationship with the Deliverer. This struggle may not be a simple or temporary limp but could be a more serious condition. God may not deliver us when we want Him to, but He does give us grace to endure our present situation until such time that He decides to deliver us.

The grace of God is sufficient for any condition and with that grace comes peace, the peace of God that surpasses all understanding! When we know God, we know peace… little God, little peace, no God, no peace. Let us be sure of our salvation before we label our struggle as a limp. Your struggle may not be unto the glory of God. Jesus said that there will be men who declare, "Lord, Lord", but He will know them not. Make your salvation sure. When I know that the Lord is my God, my Saviour, and my Deliverer, I can endure hardships as a good soldier of the cross.

Faith is… the confidence that I have in that which I cannot see, or that which has not yet been made manifest in my life.

That confidence, which is my faith, allows me to endure my temporary situation without complaints or anxiety. I know, without doubt, that in His own time I will be delivered from this limp. Faith is my gift that the Lord gives me to be able to endure whatever I am faced with or whatever I will have to endure for whatever time period He allows. When we were born we were all given *"a measure of faith"* to receive the Lord as our Saviour.

Ephesians 4:7
But unto every one of us is given grace according to the measure of the gift of Christ.

KJV Romans 12:3
according as God hath dealt to every man the measure of faith.

Following my salvation that faith should then grow continually through the trials, tests, and triumphs that the Lord places in my life. Peter wrote *"Beloved, think it not strange..."*. Paul concludes this thought with his writing of *"My grace is sufficient"*.

KJV 1 Peter 4:12-13
Beloved, think it not strange concerning the fiery trial which is to try you, as though some strange thing

happened unto you: But rejoice, inasmuch as ye are partakers of Christ's sufferings; that, when his glory shall be revealed, ye may be glad also with exceeding joy.

We have all that we need to overcome or to endure, in the person of the Holy Spirit. Jesus said, *"I pray the Father that He will send another".* (John 14:16) The third person of the Trinity, The Holy Spirit, is in us to teach us, comfort us and to bring back to our memories, the promises made to us. His presence is given to every believer that he may have the confidence required to walk this walk in righteousness. The Holy Spirit is the power that enables us to speak that which we cannot see or that which has not yet come into our reality.

Chapter Four

Jacob's Limp

In Genesis 32 we read the story of Jacob's return to face his brother. Before he was to meet up with him, the story tells us that he sent his wives, children and servants on ahead so that he is left alone. All night, Jacob wrestles with a man, whom he overcomes and will not release. He is seeking a blessing and will not let the man go until he receives what he needs. Before the breaking of day, the man touches Jacob's hip thus causing him to have a limp.

The importance of this story here is that Jacob's limp was not caused by anything he did wrong. Jacob had done many things in his past that caused him to limp spiritually, but here it is not the wrong he has done or the sin he has committed, but this time his limp is physical and is caused by his doing something right. Jacob needed a blessing from God and he was so determined to get his blessing that he wrestled with God throughout the night and refused to let go. The limp that Jacob had was physical, but it was a testimony to what the Lord had done in his life.

Jacob understood, as did the Apostle Paul, that some infirmities or some limps are given to us and are designed to remind us of God's grace.

KJV 2 Corinthians 12:9
And he said unto me, My grace is sufficient for thee: for my strength is made perfect in weakness. Most gladly therefore will I rather glory in my infirmities, that the power of Christ may rest upon me.

Jacob had seen the face of God and lived. He had wrestled with God and prevailed. He needed something that only God could provide, and he purposed in his mind and in his spirit that no matter how long he had to hang on to the Lord, he would not let go until he received his deliverance. What a powerful testimony! When we reach the point of total dependency upon God for deliverance we can grab hold to God through the vehicle of prayer and continue to hold on to Him until He blesses us. It is, sometimes, in our total frustration that we truly seek the face of God and gain the determination to hold on through the nighttime of our storms and even into the breaking of the new day. We too can grab hold to God and not let go even though it looks like a new day is breaking through.

Jacob had reached a point where he knew that only God could deliver him. He was running from his place of refuge and returning to the place he had run away from. Jacob left the place where he belonged when he wronged his brother and ran to the place that would eventually wrong him. However, he found refuge in a place where he did not belong.

When we have messed up and we leave home to run away from our wrongdoing, in time, the place we run to for refuge will become the place of our torment. Jacob's uncle Laban had covered him for years but now sought to destroy him. The trickster had been tricked by somebody who was just as tricky as he was. Now fearing for his life, he is forced to return home. Thus his conflict with his uncle chasing him from behind, his brother in front of him wanting to kill him and desert on either side of him; Jacob had nowhere to go, but to God. When he lifted up his eyes, *"up to the hills from whence cometh our help",* he saw an Angel. That Angel was the second Person of the Trinity who came to deliver him from his trials and to bless him in the presence of his enemies. That angel was also our Deliverer, who came to restore us unto Himself.

"The Angel who wrestled with Jacob was the second Person in the sacred Trinity, who was afterwards God manifest in the flesh, and who, dwelling in human nature, is called Immanuel, Hos. xii. 4, 5". (Matthew Henry)

Cheryl McGrath wrote, [2]"This is a critical moment for the corporate Bride, a season of violent abandonment and discomfort as our weakness is exposed and His all sufficiency overtakes us. As we wrestle and behold His Face, we are seeing with ever increasing clarity in the starkness of His Daybreak that truthfully without Christ we can do nothing, yet in Christ we can do ALL things. We are about to find out what that truly means.

Cry out, church of the Living God, cry out church of the Firstborn, cry and moan for His fullness as never before. Do not let Him go until we have taken hold of His very fullness and leave this place of wrestling changed and limping, leaning only on our Beloved. Cry out for His fullness until we have prevailed with Him and He changes our nature, changes our name (Rev. 2:17) and appears in all His glory in His spiritual temple! For daybreak comes and we must prevail! Selah!"

We like Jacob can also reach a point where in prayer, we can get a hold to our Deliverer, the one who died for our sins in order to keep us free from our enemy. It is so sad that the only time some of us reach out and grab hold to God is when our backs are up against the wall. Our enemies are closing in on us and we can see no way out of our situations. Like Jacob, there is trouble in front of us,

---

[2] Cheryl McGrath, http://www.greatsouthland.org/limping.html

behind us and all around us seems to be only the vastness of a desert. But when we lift up our eyes, we can find our God waiting to save us, even from ourselves. Just as Moses was told to tell the Israelites, we too can *"Look up and live"*.

KJV 2 Corinthians 12:7

And lest I should be exalted above measure through the abundance of the revelations, there was given to me a thorn in the flesh, the messenger of Satan to buffet me, lest I should be exalted above measure.

KJV 2 Corinthians 12:10

Therefore I take pleasure in infirmities, in reproaches, in necessities, in persecutions, in distresses for Christ's sake: for when I am weak, then am I strong.

Matthew Henry writes, *"Jacob halted on his thigh. It might serve to keep him from being lifted up with the abundance of the revelations."* Jacob's struggle with God and his ultimate prevailing to receive his blessing could have caused him to be lifted up with pride. The limp given to him is somewhat similar to the thorn in Paul's flesh. It serves as a reminder, that not only did he wrestle with God but also he lived to tell about it. It served to keep him humble. Concerning the account of Paul's thorn in the flesh, Matthew Henry wrote; *"The apostle gives an account of the method God took to keep him humble, and to prevent his being lifted up above measure, on account of the visions and revelations he had. We are not told what this thorn in the flesh was, whether some great trouble, or some great temptation. But God often brings this good out of evil, that the reproaches of our enemies help to hide pride from us. If God loves us, he will keep us from being exalted above measure; and spiritual burdens are ordered to cure spiritual pride.*

This thorn in the flesh is said to be a messenger of Satan, which he sent for evil; but God designed it, and overruled it for good. Prayer is a salve for every sore, a remedy for every malady; and when we are afflicted with thorns in the flesh, we should give ourselves to prayer. If an answer were not given to the first prayer, nor to the second, we are to continue praying. Troubles are sent to teach us to pray; and are continued, to teach us to continue instant in prayer. Though God accepts the prayer of faith, yet he does not always give what is asked for: as he sometimes grants in wrath, so he sometimes denies in love. When God does not take away our troubles and temptations, yet, if he gives grace enough for us, we have no reason to complain.

Grace signifies the good will of God towards us, and that is enough to enlighten and enliven us, sufficient to strengthen and comfort in all afflictions and distresses. His strength is made perfect in our weakness. Thus his grace is manifested and magnified. When we are weak in ourselves, then we are strong in the grace of our Lord Jesus Christ; when we feel that we are weak in ourselves, then we go to Christ, receive strength from him, and enjoy most the supplies of Divine strength and grace".

"Sometimes in our walk with God we find that we are spiritually limping. Our prayer life dries up. Our fear exceeds our faith; our guilt exceeds our joy. These limps occur when we don't put all our weight on God's grace".

Dr. M. Craig Barnes
The National Presbyterian Church

Chapter Five

Saved, But Limping

Grammy Award winner and anointed psalmist, Pastor Donnie McClurkin recorded a song that was entitled **"We Fall Down"**, wherein he referenced a passage from the Proverbs. The lyrics are *"We fall down but we get up, for a saint is just a sinner who fell down and got up."* He goes on to say that you can *"Get back up again"*. When you walk with a limp you are subject to fall down and sometimes more than once. The Psalmist goes on to record that even though we may fall down, we shall not be destroyed or *"utterly cast down"*, because the Lord of Hosts himself will hold us upright in His hands.

KJV Proverbs 24:16
For a just man falleth seven times, and riseth up again: but the wicked shall fall into mischief.

Psalms 37:24

Though he fall, he shall not be utterly cast down: for the Lord upholdeth him with his hand.

Micah 7:8

Rejoice not against me, O mine enemy: when I fall, I shall arise; when I sit in darkness, the Lord shall be a light unto me.

The recording caused quite a stir in the church community. There were those who rejected this thought very strongly, as though they themselves have never stumbled. We must be careful that we do not set ourselves up as judge and jury over the shortcomings of others, for we ourselves may find trouble on it's way to our door. In every instance, in the Scriptures when Jesus was confronted with a sinner in need of deliverance, He healed them and instructed them to go and sin no more.

We are also to forgive our brothers and sisters when they fall, slip, or limp. Jesus said to Peter that we are to forgive our brother even seventy times seven. If we were not subject to slipping, falling or sinning, it would not be necessary for us to forgive a fellow brother or sister, for there would be nothing to forgive them for.

Some Christians are limping due to what we have come to know as *"church hurt"*, but yet again this is another area where forgiveness and the grace of God is to be exhibited. We must get over what happened to us in our past, in our lives, and in the church, if we are to do the will of God. Susan Sealy wrote, [3]"We allow wounds inside to fester without seeking help or handling them according to biblical principles. Consequently, we often carry the hurts longer than we need to. We adjust our routines and attitudes to accommodate the injury as if it has taken up permanent residence in our souls. And that puts a big burden on the people around us who have to tiptoe around our skewed sensitivities. We allow relationships to become strained. Rather than embracing the hope, healing, and forgiveness in the Lord, we use our disappointment to justify spiritually limping along. We tire easier and give up quicker on running the race that's set before us as

Christians because, after all, as we explain to ourselves, "We've been burned."

KJV Matthew 18:21-22

Then came Peter to him, and said, Lord, how oft shall my brother sin against me, and I forgive him? Till seven times? Jesus saith unto him, I say not unto thee, Until seven times: but, Until seventy times seven.

Matthew Henry wrote, *"The greatness of sin magnifies the riches of pardoning mercy; and the comfortable sense of pardoning mercy, does much to dispose our hearts to forgive our brethren."*

Apostle Paul wrote in Romans *"For all have sinned, and come short of the glory of God."* It is interesting that he does not say *"have come"* or *"fallen"*, which would indicate past tense. By using the present tense here he is saying that we yet come short of God's glory. None of us are perfect and therefore subject to falling into sin or as we

---

[3] Susan Sealy, Assistant Pastor The Believer's Church Tulsa, OK

say stumbling.

The phrase *"come short"*, as referenced in the Strong's Dictionary is Ref. # 5302.

> • ***Romanized: hustereo; Pronounced hoos-ter-eh'-o from GSN5306; to be later, i.e. (by implication) to be inferior; generally, to fall short (be deficient): KJV--come behind (short), be destitute, fail, lack, suffer need, (be in) want, be the worse.***

As we look at the original meaning of the phrase, can we not all be described as being either destitute, in lack, in want, inferior, deficient, or have suffered or just been worse at one time or another in our Christian walk? Can we not all fit into this category?

This question was asked of the people of God by the prophet Elijah centuries ago and is still being asked today:

1 Kings 18:21

Spiritually Limping

"And Elijah came near unto all the people, and said, How long go ye limping between the two sides? If Jehovah be God, follow him; but if Baal, then follow him. And the people answered him not a word." -- American Standard

1 Kings 18:21

"Elijah went before the people and said, "How long will you waver between two opinions? If the LORD is God, follow him; but if Baal is God, follow him." But the people said nothing." -- New International

Matthew Henry's Concise Commentary explains the above passage this way. *"Many of the people wavered in their judgment, and varied in their practice. Elijah called upon them to determine whether Jehovah or Baal was the self-existent, supreme God, the Creator, Governor, and Judge of the world, and to follow him alone.* ***It is dangerous to halt between the service of God and the service of sin, the dominion of Christ and the dominion of our lusts****. If Jesus be the only Saviour, let us cleave to him alone for every thing; if the Bible be the world of God, let us*

Spiritually Limping

reverence and receive the whole of it, and submit our understanding to the Divine teaching it contains."

"How long go ye limping between the two sides?" If where you are today is limping, let it not be between the serving of God and the serving of the flesh. Too many of those who are working in the house of the Lord are not just limping but indeed limping between the two sides of... *"Whether God be God or Baal be god".*

When it was announced that the war to free Iraq was won, many soldiers rejoiced, but many were later killed because the war itself was not over. There are still many scrimmages to be fought before we can declare the war over. Many of the saints today rejoice because the word of God tells us that battle is already won. We often times forget that there will yet be scrimmages that we must still fight. The writer of the book of Ephesians tells us that as we prepare to continue to fight, there is something that will not be done for us, but something that we must do for ourselves. We must *prepare* ourselves for battle.

KJV Ephesians 6:11-18

11. "Put on the whole armour of God, that ye may be able to stand against the wiles of the devil.

12. For we wrestle not against flesh and blood, but against principalities, against powers, against the rulers of the darkness of this world, against spiritual wickedness in high places.

13. Wherefore take unto you the whole armour of God, that ye may be able to withstand in the evil day, and having done all, to stand.

14. Stand therefore, having your loins girt about with truth, and having on the breastplate of righteousness;

15. And your feet shod with the preparation of the gospel of peace;

16. Above all, taking the shield of faith, wherewith ye shall be able to quench all the fiery darts of the wicked.

17. And take the helmet of salvation, and the sword of the Spirit, which is the word of God:

18. Praying always with all prayer and supplication in the Spirit, and watching thereunto with all perseverance and supplication for all saints;"

Spiritually Limping

Are you limping today simply because you have failed to prepare yourself for the battles that you have faced or will one day face? We have all been given the equipment we need to war against our enemies, but we must *"PUT IT ON"!* Having a raincoat in your car, closet, or at home will not keep you dry when it is raining... You have to put it on. When we were children, our parents dressed us protectively, but as we became adults, we then became responsible for dressing ourselves, protectively. The same applies in the spirit.

We are so blessed to live in a time when everything we need is readily available to us. Not only can we receive the Word at church on Sunday, but also with all of our electronic and technological advancements, we can take that same Word home with us, in our cars and even on our jobs. We have 24-hour Christian television and radio, as well as, books, audio and videotapes available almost anywhere. The Bible says in Roman 10:17 that *"faith cometh by hearing"* and today we have the capability to continually hear a word that can help build up our faith. But just as with the raincoat, if we do not use what we have at our disposal, we will be unprotected, getting soaked by the elements, bringing sickness and harm upon ourselves.

The Christian Armor is made to be worn; and there is no putting off our armor till we have done our warfare, and finished our course." (Matthew Henry)

Chapter Six

The Problem Is With Us

2 Chronicles 7:14

If my people, which are called by my name, shall humble themselves, and pray, and seek my face, and turn from their wicked ways; then will I hear from heaven, and will forgive their sin, and will heal their land.

In 2nd Chronicles chapter 7, we find God's answer to the prayer of Solomon concerning the consecration of the House of the Lord that was built and dedicated by Solomon. God responds to Solomon's prayer by saying to him that **HE HAS HEARD HIS PRAYER.** What an awesome statement! You do know that God still hears and answers prayer today. For those who do not spend time praying to God concerning our situations, we are missing the one vital link to resolving our problems. Only God can fix whatever is wrong in your life and the only way to take your problem to him is through prayer.

Solomon with all of his wisdom, riches, wealth and power was a praying man. Some of us get a good or decent job, get a little money in the bank, start driving a new car and we literally lose our minds. We stop doing the one thing that it took to get us from the cotton fields, the factories, and the kitchens to where we are today. **AND THAT IS TO HUMBLE OURSELVES AND PRAY!**

James 5:16

"The effectual fervent prayer of a righteous man availeth much."

So as God answers Solomon's prayer in verse 13; and says *" If I shut up heaven that there be no rain, or if I command the locusts to devour the land, or if I send pestilence among my people;"*. Here, God is saying that there will be some times when He may be the cause of our afflictions. Now, I know that most of us would love to believe that everything that comes against us is the work of Satan. We need to stop trying to rebuke the Lord by calling what He is allowing, the work of the enemy. You do remember that the Apostle Paul said in... ***2 Corinthians 12:7-10*** *that there was given to him a thorn in his flesh and 3 times he asked the Lord to take it away, but He responded by saying that My Grace Is Sufficient for Thee.*

Why is it that most Christians think that they should be exempt from sufferings, problems, trials and tribulations? If Christ suffered persecution, surely you know that we will suffer too. Paul wrote in... ***2 Corinthians 4:17-18*** *"For our light affliction, which is but for a moment, worketh for us a far more exceeding and eternal weight of glory; While we look not at the things, which are seen, but at the things, which are not seen: for the things, which are, seen are temporal; but the things which are not seen are eternal."*

God told Solomon that no matter what I allow to come against My people; which are called by my name, (*if they would first*) humble themselves (*secondly*) and pray, and seek my face, (*thirdly*) and turn from their wicked ways;

then will I hear from heaven, and will forgive their sin, and will heal their land.

Take notice here that there are 3 things that you have to do. *(One for the Father, One for the Son and One for the Holy Ghost.) For us to hear from heaven, be forgiven and receive healing, we need to get the Trinity.* We need the Creative work of The Father, the Redeeming work of the Son and the Sustaining work of The Holy Spirit! We need all 3!

This is a binding contractual agreement that God is willing to enter into with anyone that is called by **HIS NAME! BUT it is conditional!**

First, the only people who can enter into this agreement must be called by His name. Let's look at what it means to be called by His name. You know that there is something about being associated with the right name. There are some perks that we can get whether we have earned them or not, if we have the right name. There are some things that you enjoy today because of whose name you bear.

Spirituality Limping

Some people marry into a name that moves them from poverty to wealth. Some people can use a name to get into places where they would normally not be allowed... *you know we call them namedroppers.* Some of us have jobs today not because of our skills or our resume' but because of whose name we know. But what's in a name?

The Bible says that at the name of Jesus, demons tremble, the sick are healed and the dead is raised again to live. When you put the right name on something, you can always get a response. If you don't believe me, try calling a church member late at night and tell them that you are calling *for* the Pastor and watch the change in their attitudes. If you know the right name, you can get stopped by the police but still not get the ticket. If you know the right name you can get away with not paying your dues in the workplace and in society.

Knowing the right name is good... it's real good, but ***Having*** the right name is even better. Knowing a Rockefeller might get you a meeting at the bank, but being a Rockefeller can get the bank to come to you. Just knowing the president might get you a visit to the White House, but being the president... entitles you to live in the White House. Just knowing the name of Jesus might cause some demons to flee, but having the name of Jesus will cause those same demons to flee and not return. For there is no other name under the earth by which man can be saved... and if that name can save me surely, being called by that same name can cause God to respond to me.

God is not talking about those so-called Christians, those people who rent the name on Sunday and return it on Monday; but He is talking to those who are called by His name **EVERYDAY**. You have got to have His name in order to enter into this contractual agreement. As the saints of old used to say, *You have got to know Him for yourself.* Too many of us are trying to access the power of God or get to God on what somebody else said or on somebody else's faith. It does not work that way in fact, it's a good way to be defeated.

KJV Acts 19:11-17

Spiritually Limping

11. "And God wrought special miracles by the hands of Paul:"

12. So that from his body were brought unto the sick handkerchiefs or aprons, and the diseases departed from them, and the evil spirits went out of them.

13. Then certain of the vagabond Jews, exorcists, took upon them to call over them which had evil spirits the name of the Lord Jesus, saying, We adjure you by Jesus whom Paul preacheth.

14. And there were seven sons of one Sceva, a Jew, and chief of the priests, which did so.

15. And the evil spirit answered and said, Jesus I know, and Paul I know; but who are ye?

16. And the man in whom the evil spirit was leaped on them, and overcame them, and prevailed against them, so that they fled out of that house naked and wounded.

17. And this was known to all the Jews and Greeks also dwelling at Ephesus; and fear fell on them all, and the name of the Lord Jesus was magnified.

Secondly, God said that if they will just **Seek MY FACE**. *Not My Hand, but MY FACE*. A problem in our modern day churches is that we want the things of God without having the God of the things. When most Christians pray, it is not according to His will, but according to our will or our needs. We have tried, whether purposely or not, to reduce God to that of a Santa Claus or a Sugar Daddy. When my granddaughter's birthday is getting close, her conduct begins to improve. She wants to receive something from us and she begins to do the things that she knows we approve of. But shortly after her birthday and after she has gotten what she wanted, she then returns to her normal behavior. This is what most of us in the Church do today.

When we need God to do something special for us, we start doing the things that would please Him. But shortly after our prayers are answered and we get what we asked for, we return to our old ways. This is why Satan is not disturbed by our coming to church, dancing, singing and shouting or by our manufactured and convenient praise. Because he knows that as soon as we get what we want from God, we are going to return to our same old wicked ways. ***And then we wonder why this world is in the condition it is in.***

God goes on to tell Solomon that after we, who are called by His name **Pray** and **Seek** His Face we still have to do something else. We have to **TURN** from our wicked ways. ***It's all ONE condition!*** Turning is not an option that we can add on if we feel like we need to. It's not like adding optional features like a CD player or cruise control on a new car. ***Turning*** is like getting a transmission to go along with the motor. Without a transmission the car will start, the air will blow, the heat will work, the radio and the lights will all come on, but the car still won't move.

I know that some of you might think that I missed something else here, that I left off a part of what God said, but I didn't forget it. I left it for later because I think that it is the main reason why most of us cannot **TURN**. Look back at the verse… First, God says that if My people who are called by My Name would do what? **HUMBLE THEMSELVES!** I believe that the main reason we cannot turn from our wicked ways, Pray and Seek God's face is that we cannot or are not willing to Humble ourselves.

These generations of churchgoers are so lifted up in pride that we have convinced ourselves that we can add to the church by holding *"**Power Meetings**"* or *"**Planning Sessions**"* and get together and strategize on what it would take to go out and recruit more members. If we get more television time, wear certain colors, get some more radio time or invite the *"Right"* people to come and speak at our church and to host those *"Concerts",* then we can be the *Church of What's Happening Now! The Greater Mt. We Got It Going On Missionary Baptist, Church of God In Christ, Methodist, Apostolic, Christian Center, Church of the World.* We have forgotten that Jesus said, *"if I be lifted Up, I'll Draw All Men Unto Me"* (KJV John 12:32).

Some of us act as though the Holy Spirit will not move unless we are leading the song or preaching the sermon, the ushers can't usher unless I am there and the deacons can't pray without me. We walk around acting like God meets with us in a One-on-One Power Meeting before He does anything and if we don't know about it first, then it could not be God. And if God should allow one of us to operate in any one of the *"Gifts of the Spirit"*, we can become insufferable. How soon we forget that it was not because we deserved His favor, but it's because, as Bishop T. D. Jakes said; *"Favor Ain't Fair"*. So, get down off your high horse and stop strutting around like somebody died and made you king, because none of us are worthy of all the things that God allows us to receive. The Apostle Paul wrote, "For a*ll have sinned, and come short of the glory of God." (Romans3:23)* .

Proverbs 16:18 says *"Pride goeth before destruction, and an haughty spirit before a fall."* I submit to you that there will be enough "falls" in your life without you adding to them by having a haughty spirit. God said that **we**, *the ones who are called by His name* had to Humble ourselves. As the children used to say… *"You better check yourself, before you wreck yourself"!*

We had better come to the realization that God does not need any of us. We all need to TURN away from something... **and** God says it is our wicked ways. Now, whether your wicked way is lying or backbiting, pride or fornication, whether it is cheating or homosexuality; regardless to what your limping is from, it does not matter... *You Still Have To Turn! Stop trying to judge somebody else and take a good look at yourself. The problem just might be with You!*

Acts 2:38

"Then Peter said unto them, Repent, and be baptized every one of you in the name of Jesus Christ for the remission of sins, and ye shall receive the gift of the Holy Ghost."

To turn means to repent. To repent literally means to change your mind, your purpose and your direction... it means to turn from one thing and head in another direction. So what God was saying even back in Solomon's days is the same thing that Jesus said in Matthew 4:17..."*Repent: for the kingdom of Heaven is at hand*". When the Kingdom of Heaven comes, our sins are forgiven and our land is healed. It's the same promise, **but**

the problem is with us. We have not lived up to our part of the agreement. God is waiting to heal our land and forgive our sins, but we have not humbled ourselves, prayed seeking His face and we definitely have not turned from our wicked ways.

Revelation 3:15-16
I know thy works, that thou art neither cold nor hot: I would thou wert cold or hot. So then because thou art lukewarm, and neither cold nor hot, I will spue thee out of my mouth.

God knows our works and he knows that we are neither hot nor cold toward Him and if we stay this way, He is going to spit us out and then we will be left behind. I don't know about you but I want to go back with Him when He comes.

He is coming back for a church without spot or wrinkle… *How will He find you? Will you be found Spotless? Or will He find you Wrinkled or Limping?* Today is the only time that we have because tomorrow is not promised to any of us... You had better get it right now, before it's too late! Saints of God, members of the Body of Christ... we are going to have some rough times and weeping may endure through the night, but joy will come in the morning light... so be not dismayed whatever betides... God will take care of you. Beneath His wings of love abide... God will take care of you.... If you just hold on through the night, hang on and don't give up... just keep on fasting, keep on praying and keep on believing and He will come to see about you.

Spiritually Limping

"*A*re you limping around with a spiritual problem? Let God deal with it! Many times there are things in our lives that cause spiritual "pain" or hindrance. Rather than allow the Lord to remove the problem, we try to limp or tiptoe around – afraid it could be too painful if we were to allow the Lord to remedy the situation."

First Lady Michelle Hancock
Apostolic Faith Church
Eureka, CA

Chapter Seven

RESTORATION

God is in the business of restoration!

KJV Isaiah 57:18-19

18. I have seen his ways, and will heal him: I will lead him also, and restore comforts unto him and to his mourners.
19. I create the fruit of the lips; Peace, peace to him that is far off, and to him that is near, saith the Lord; and I will heal him.

KJV Jeremiah 30:17

17. For I will restore health unto thee, and I will heal thee of thy wounds, saith the Lord; because they called thee an Outcast, saying, This is Zion, whom no man seeketh after.

Spiritually Limping

KJV Joel 2:23-27

23. Be glad then, ye children of Zion, and rejoice in the Lord your God: for he hath given you the former rain moderately, and he will cause to come down for you the rain, the former rain, and the latter rain in the first month.

24. And the floors shall be full of wheat, and the fats shall overflow with wine and oil.

25. And I will restore to you the years that the locust hath eaten, the cankerworm, and the caterpillar, and the palmerworm, my great army which I sent among you.

26. And ye shall eat in plenty, and be satisfied, and praise the name of the Lord your God, that hath dealt wondrously with you: and my people shall never be ashamed.

27. And ye shall know that I am in the midst of Israel, and that I am the Lord your God, and none else: and my people shall never be ashamed.

KJV Matthew 12:13

13. Then saith he to the man, Stretch forth thine hand. And he stretched it forth; and it was restored whole, like as the other.

Spiritually Limping

KJV Mark 8:25

25. After that he put his hands again upon his eyes, and made him look up: and he was restored, and saw every man clearly.

Limping is what many Christians are doing daily but unfortunately this is a subject that the church has been very reluctant to deal with. Until we face the truth of the struggles that many of us face there will be no healing and the church will continue to suffer. For when one member of the body is in pain the whole body will also feel the effects of that pain. Richard Smallwood sings *"don't be discouraged... there is healing for your sorrow, healing for your pain, healing for your spirit, there's shelter from the rain"*. He goes on to say that *"there is a balm in Gilead to make the wounded whole"*. Jesus Christ is that balm and with his strips we are already healed.

KJV Isaiah 53:4-5

4. Surely he hath borne our griefs, and carried our sorrows: yet we did esteem him stricken, smitten of God, and afflicted.

5. But he was wounded for our transgressions, he was bruised for our iniquities: the chastisement of our peace was upon him; and with his stripes we are healed.

Healing for whatever affliction we may have has already been given to the saints, all we have to do is claim our healing. The Lord God our Father is an omniscient God, therefore he knows everything there is to know about us. He knew us before we were formed in our mother's womb and he also knows our end. God is never surprised at anything that we have done or will do in the future. Our faults, flaws and shortcomings are not unexpected by him. The Scriptures record that *His Grace is sufficient for us.*

God can and does use us even with all of our faults. As we study the Bible we see that many of the mighty moves of God were worked through men of faults, people with a limp. The woman at the well, whom Jesus used to bring the good news to an entire town, was a woman with a limp. David limped, Moses limped, Abraham limped and Sarah limped, just as many of us limp. We must come to understand that the Lord is well able to take our weak flesh, clean us up and then use us mightily in the work of the Kingdom. God knows each and every one of us and when we submit ourselves to His will and come to Him in all honesty and without pretence, He can and will clean us up and use us in His work.

Donnie McClurkin sings a song that asks the question *"How do you handle the guilt of your past?"* His answer is*:* **"You Just Stand."** He says *"after you have done all you can, you just stand and be sure, be not entangled in that bondage again… God has a purpose, yes God has a plan"*. **That is the key! Knowing that God has a purpose and a plan!**

All we have to do is continue on, submitting ourselves to His will… coming to Him just as we are and then letting Him do the work. If we were able to clean ourselves of all our messes, we would not need a God. Acknowledge where you are and go on and in His divine timing, He will do what is necessary.

Another of our problems is that we can convince ourselves that our limp is not as bad as it is, or that others cannot see it. Just as drunk drivers convinces themselves that they can drive just as well drinking as when they are sober, we also deceive ourselves that our limp does not cause our walk to be staggered or irregular. When the drunk driver is pulled over by the police, they are often given a test that will require them to walk a straight line. This is not done to prove to the officer that they cannot do it, but so that the drivers can see for themselves that they are staggering.

God has to sometimes allow us to be pulled aside and tested in our walk, in order that we can see that, yes, others can see that our walk is jerky, irregular or unsteady. When we attempt to hide our limp, when in fact, many others can see us limping, the covers must then be pulled off and we must be exposed in order that we acknowledge our shortcomings and then seek healing and restoration. Trying to hide our limp is not the way to seek or receive healing or restoration. Restoration can only come when we recognize where we are in this walk and openly confess our sins before the Lord, repent and seek His forgiveness.

Spiritually Limping

In the story of the prodigal son who found himself in a place, far from where he should have been, far from the father who loved him and unable to undo the damage that he himself had created, the Bible says, *"he came to himself"* (Luke 15). We have to come to ourselves and acknowledge that we have a father who has more than enough mercy, grace, love and compassion to restore us to our rightful place in Him. All we have to do is get up and go home and He will do the rest. The question comes to mind… do we stop working, do we sit down and wait until the Lord has restored us? What are we to do while we are struggling to get back home? I believe that the answer is we keep on keeping on… even if we have to limp all the way back to our rightful place.

There will be times in your walk that you will be tempted to just give up, because of your limp. You can begin to feel and think that there is no way that God could ever use you in the condition that you are in and you may have embarrassed yourself and feel like you have also embarrassed God, but before you give up, before you throw in the towel, remember how God forgave and

Spiritually Limping

restored his disciple, Peter. Peter denied Christ just before He was crucified and when he realized that the word of Jesus, to him on this matter, had actually come to pass; the Bible says, *"he wept bitterly"*. But the account goes on to let us know that when Jesus was resurrected he not only sent word to his disciples, but he specified Peter. Our restoration is assured, even in our limping, when we are in our rightful place in God. Yes, we will sin and fall short sometimes, but if we repent and seek His forgiveness, we can and will be restored.

KJV Matthew 26:33-35

33. Peter answered and said unto him, Though all men shall be offended because of thee, yet will I never be offended.
34. Jesus said unto him, Verily I say unto thee, That this night, before the cock crow, thou shalt deny me thrice.
35. Peter said unto him, Though I should die with thee, yet will I not deny thee.

KJV Matthew 26:69-75

Spiritually Limping

69. Now Peter sat without in the palace: and a damsel came unto him, saying, Thou also wast with Jesus of Galilee.

70. But he denied before them all, saying, I know not what thou sayest.

71. And when he was gone out into the porch, another maid saw him, and said unto them that were there, This fellow was also with Jesus of Nazareth.

72. And again he denied with an oath, I do not know the man.

73. And after a while came unto him they that stood by, and said to Peter, Surely thou also art one of them; for thy speech bewrayeth thee.

74. Then began he to curse and to swear, saying, I know not the man. And immediately the cock crew.

75. And Peter remembered the word of Jesus, which said unto him, Before the cock crow, thou shalt deny me thrice. And he went out, and wept bitterly.

KJV Mark 16:7

6. *But go your way, tell his disciples and Peter that he goeth before you into Galilee: there shall ye see him, as he said unto you.*

God is never taken by surprise by our faults or our failures. He is an all-knowing, all wise, and forgiving God, and He knew us, and every mistake we would make before He ever called us. We must remember that it was He that called us and not us who called ourselves to Him. While we had to choose Him, we could only choose Him because of that measure of faith that He gave to us... in order that we could choose Him.

KJV John 15:16

16. Ye have not chosen me, but I have chosen you, and ordained you, that ye should go and bring forth fruit, and that your fruit should remain: that whatsoever ye shall ask of the Father in my name, he may give it you.

KJV Ephesians 1:4-8

4. According as he hath chosen us in him before the foundation of the world, that we should be holy and without blame before him in love:

5. Having predestinated us unto the adoption of children by Jesus Christ to himself, according to the good pleasure of his will,

6. To the praise of the glory of his grace, wherein he hath made us accepted in the beloved.

7. In whom we have redemption through his blood, the forgiveness of sins, according to the riches of his grace;

8. Wherein he hath abounded toward us in all wisdom and prudence;

In the book of Acts on the Day of Pentecost, Peter is found preaching with such power and anointing that many who heard him were saved and came to the same Christ that they had crucified. The anointing rested on Peter so heavily that the mere falling of his shadow on the sick brought about healing. When Peter denied Jesus before the crucifixion that was a limp in his walk that caused him to hide out in shame and fear. God's plan for Peter included his time of limping. Peter stands now as an example of the power that we can receive by the Holy Spirit regardless to what we have done.

KJV Acts 5:14-16

13. And believers were the more added to the Lord, multitudes both of men and women.)

14. Insomuch that they brought forth the sick into the streets, and laid them on beds and couches, that at the least

15. the shadow of Peter passing by might overshadow some of them.

16. There came also a multitude out of the cities round about unto Jerusalem, bringing sick folks, and them which were vexed with unclean spirits: and they were healed every one.

The great Apostle Paul wrote that in our flesh there is no good thing. (Romans 7:18) Therefore, if I am operating in my flesh, there is nothing good that can come from my work. However if I am operating in the Spirit of the living God, my work will be of Him and not of me. It is the Lord's business and His alone whom He chooses to work through and if He chooses to work through me while I am limping, that too is His business. I cannot stop being available to Him and just sit around waiting on my deliverance. I may have to operate while I am limping in order that some other person who may be limping can see the goodness of the Lord in me.

The key here is that I must be sure that it is the Lord operating in me and not me in my flesh. Operating in my flesh I can cause others to stumble and fall and then their blood will be on my hands. First I must be sure that my relationship with the Father is in tact. I must know without doubt that the Lord Jesus Christ is my Saviour and that it is in His Spirit that I speak, move and operate. When I understand who God is and who I am in Him, then and only then can I be effective.

Without this understanding I may find myself trying to do His work on my own and it is then that I will fail and cause others to fall. I must be in an intimate relationship with Him first and then I can expect restoration. Without an intimate relationship with Him, to attempt to do the work of the Kingdom, I will be counted among those to whom the Lord will say, Depart from me, I know you not.

KJV Matthew 7:21-27

21. Not every one that saith unto me, Lord, Lord, shall enter into the kingdom of heaven; but he that doeth the will of my Father which is in heaven.

22. Many will say to me in that day, Lord, Lord, have we not prophesied in thy name? and in thy name have cast out devils? and in thy name done many wonderful works?

23. And then will I profess unto them, I never knew you: depart from me, ye that work iniquity.

24. Therefore whosoever heareth these sayings of mine, and doeth them, I will liken him unto a wise man, which built his house upon a rock:

25. And the rain descended, and the floods came, and the winds blew, and beat upon that house; and it fell not: for it was founded upon a rock.

26. And every one that heareth these sayings of mine, and doeth them not, shall be likened unto a foolish man, which built his house upon the sand:

27. *And the rain descended, and the floods came, and the winds blew, and beat upon that house; and it fell: and great was the fall of it.*

When we are positive that the hand of the Lord is upon us we can then operate in His power and see results that will be pleasing to Him. One sure sign that you are not operating to the glory of the Lord is when you are receiving the glory. It seems to be so easy for some of the saints to get caught up in the situation of stealing God's glory. When what you do is to your benefit, your gain, your profit… it is not of God.

The prophet Ezekiel wrote in chapter 37 that the hand of the Lord was upon him and carried him to an uncomfortable place, a place of death and loss and then placed before him what would appear to be an impossible task. God sometimes places some of us in uncomfortable situations with what appears to be impossible tasks. Ours is only to do His will, not to understand it all… and then God gets the glory when the task is completed.

Ezekiel was positioned to make something happen that only God could achieve. Because Ezekiel knew that it was the hand of the Lord upon him and that it was the Lord's Spirit that moved him to this place, then he also knew that the Lord would accomplish whatever tasks set before him.

It was not in his own power that the prophet spoke to the bones, but in the power of the Lord.

God sometimes places us in uncomfortable surrounding with tasks that can seem impossible, but when we know that it is the Lord orchestrating our moves, we can do what is required and without complaint or fear. It is then that restoration can come to the body and God should be the only one receiving the glory. Our own restoration may be linked directly to the restoration of somebody else. Ezekiel's prophesy was to the children of Israel who was at this time in captivity in Babylon. This captivity was in fact their second deportation. While this prophecy was due to the sin of the nation, it yet addresses the individual sin of each of us.

Dr. Stanley L. Morris says this: *"God had to punish His people because of His hatred for idolatry, but He never ceased to love them. Judah's sin was a national one, but Ezekiel also stressed individual responsibility for one's own sins to an extent unparalleled in the rest of the Old Testament".*

Ezekiel was not a part of the problem, but yet he was one of the captives. When the Lord punishes the house for corporate sin, there will be those of us who may suffer with the house, even though we are not participants. It may be that the Lord will use you to bring restoration to the whole house, so don't despair and begin to blame where you are on the wrong doings of others. Your suffering may be in the will of the Lord.

KJV Romans 8:28

28. And we know that all things work together for good to them that love God, to them who are the called according to his purpose.

That encompasses the good times but it also includes some bad times.

Matthew Henry's Concise Commentary explains the above passage this way: *"Every providence tends to the spiritual good of those that love God; in breaking them off from sin, bringing them nearer to God, weaning them from the world, and fitting them for heaven. When the saints act out of character, corrections will be employed to bring them back again."*

As saints we consistently quote Romans 8:28, but realistically we never expect anything other than good things to happen to us. When the bad things or the inconvenient things happen, most saints fall into a pity party and begin to beg God for deliverance. When will the church grow up and try, first to get an understanding of what is going on and what God's purpose is in this. Many of us who are limping may find that restoration will come much faster if we would only stop long enough to seek God in every situation we face. Every pain or suffering is not always about you. When Jesus suffered and was crucified, it was not about him... it was for all of us. As Jesus is our example we also will have to suffer for the sake of others. However, rest in the promises of the Lord that all of these things will work together for our good.

When we stop dealing with the symptoms and begin to address the cause, we will understand that there are some things we must go through. We cannot always go around the obstacles in our lives; there are some that we will just have to face. In order to get up, Jesus had to first go down.

When you look at your situation, condition, health and station in life or whatever... Stop looking at what is! Instead look at what is to be, where you are in your relationship with the Lord and His promises to you. When you focus on your condition you are focused on the symptoms and not on the cause. When we cough that is a symptom. When we treat the cough and not the cause of the cough, it may go away for a while, but it will return because we have not treated the cause of the cough. If you are bleeding, you have got to look pass the blood and find the *cause* of the bleeding. If you only treat the symptom and not the cause, it may lead to a greater problem. When we see people limping, we only see the symptom, but in order for them to receive deliverance we must address the cause of the limp.

For far too long the church has been handing out canes, crutches, walkers and wheel chairs to people who are limping within the body of Christ. The time has come for the church to see a limping saint and know that the limp is only a symptom of something greater and begin to focus on the cause and not on the symptom.

A saint should never stop his walk because he is limping, the limp must be dealt with. Some limps can only be resolved over a period of time, some will require corrective action, some will require a one-on-one consultation with the Great Physician and some are given as an indication of an encounter with One who is more powerful and no further action can be taken.

Regardless to what it looks like when we limp, our main concern cannot be placed on the limp. We must focus our attention, our prayers and our minds on what the limping is a result of. If we find that there is a problem, then solve the problem. If we find that the limping is a result of divine intervention, then we must do nothing. Judging somebody else's limp is a dangerous thing to do. Acceptance of each other is the only action that we must take unless otherwise directed by the Holy One Himself.

For far too long, many of us have <u>attributed to Satan the work of the Lord.</u> We are too quick to call what God is doing, an attack of the enemy, only because we have not sought God for direction in the situation. So, while many are limping, who are we as individuals to pass judgment on where they are in their walk with the Lord. This can cause many to stop walking when the Lord was actually ordering their steps.

Unless we have been given divine insight into the cause of the limp of our fellow brother or sister, we should keep silent and pray for them. Until you have lived through my struggle, please do not attempt to judge me. In our own case, when we are limping, let us seek God for direction

Spirituality Limping

and an answer as to why we are in the condition we find ourselves in today.

When Job appeared to be limping, his friends and his wife judged him and were found to be wrong. How would you like to have been one of his friends? What would your assessment of Job's situation have been? We must be careful trying to assess a situation without all of the facts, both known and unknown. Job appeared to be limping, when in fact he was given up to Satan as an example of a true and upright man.

God trusted Job in this situation; can He trust you with trials when everybody around you is trying to judge what is going on? Daniel was held in captivity and told to worship the king or die. Standing before the lion's den, it might have appeared to some his walk had a slight limp, but he stood on what he knew of His God and declared that God was able to deliver him whether He did or not.

KJV Colossians 2:1-10

Spiritually Limping

1. For I would that ye knew what great conflict I have for you, and for them at Laodicea, and for as many as have not seen my face in the flesh;

2. That their hearts might be comforted, being knit together in love, and unto all riches of the full assurance of understanding, to the acknowledgement of the mystery of God, and of the Father, and of Christ;

3. In whom are hid all the treasures of wisdom and knowledge.

4.And this I say, lest any man should beguile you with enticing words.

5. For though I be absent in the flesh, yet am I with you in the spirit, joying and beholding your order, and the stedfastness of your faith in Christ.

6. As ye have therefore received Christ Jesus the Lord, so walk ye in him:

7. Rooted and built up in him, and stablished in the faith, as ye have been taught, abounding therein with thanksgiving.

8. Beware lest any man spoil you through philosophy and vain deceit, after the tradition of men, after the rudiments of the world, and not after Christ.

9. For in him dwelleth all the fulness of the Godhead bodily.

10. And ye are complete in him, which is the head of all principality and power:

Matthew Henry's Concise Commentary gives the following revelation on the above passage:

"The soul prospers when we have clear knowledge of the truth as it is in Jesus. When we not only believe with the heart, but are ready, when called, to make confession with the mouth. Knowledge and faith make a soul rich. The stronger our faith, and the warmer our love, the more will our comfort be. The treasures of wisdom are hid, not from us, but for us, in Christ. These were hid from proud unbelievers, but displayed in the person and redemption of Christ. See the danger of enticing words; how many are ruined by the false disguises and fair appearances of evil principles and wicked practices! Be aware and afraid of those who would entice to any evil; for they aim to spoil you. All Christians have, in profession at least, received Jesus Christ the Lord, consented to him, and taken him for

theirs. We cannot be built up in Christ, or grow in him, unless we are first rooted in him, or founded upon him.

Being established in the faith, we must abound therein, and improve in it more and more. God justly withdraws this benefit from those who do not receive it with thanksgiving; and God justly requires gratitude for his mercies.

There is a philosophy, which rightly exercises our reasonable faculties; a study of the works of God, which leads us to the knowledge of God, and confirms our faith in him. But there is a philosophy which is vain and deceitful; and while it pleases men's fancies, hinders their faith: such are curious speculations about things above us, or no concern to us. Those who walk in the way of the world, are turned from following Christ. We have in Him the substance of all the shadows of the ceremonial law. All the defects of it are made up in the gospel of Christ, by his complete sacrifice for sin, and by the revelation of the will of God. To be complete, is to be furnished with all things necessary for salvation. By this one word "complete," is shown that we have in Christ whatever is required. "In him," not when we look to Christ, as though he were distant from us, but we are in him, when, by the power of the Spirit, we have faith wrought in our hearts by the Spirit, and we are united to our Head."

In all the things that will come to us and/or against us, our faith and understanding of God and how He works is the one thing that will sustain us. In order to walk this walk of Christendom, with or without a limp we must first be sure that we are *"in Christ Jesus"*. Our certainty in our relationship is the only thing that we need to know for sure, and God will handle all the rest. There is an old saying that if you take care of the things of God, He will take care of you.

KJV Isaiah 26:3-4
3. Thou wilt keep him in perfect peace, whose mind is stayed on thee: because he trusteth in thee.
4. Trust ye in the Lord for ever: for in the Lord Jehovah is everlasting strength:

Spiritually Limping

Matthew Henry expounds thusly, *"Thou wilt keep him in peace; in perfect peace, inward peace, outward peace, peace with God, peace of conscience, peace at all times, in all events. Trust in the Lord for that peace, that portion, which will be for ever. Whatever we trust to the world for, it will last only for a moment; but those who trust in God shall not only find in him, but shall receive from him, strength that will carry them to that blessedness which is for ever. Let us then acknowledge him in all our ways, and rely on him in all trials."*

It is only God's business what He allows us to encounter. If we are limping as a punishment, take your punishment and keep on going. If He is using us as a testimony to others, endure with gladness the test, and keep on walking. Even if you don't understand what God is doing or why you are limping… Keep on Walking until He reveals the reason to you.

In every case, when we keep on walking… God will get the Glory!

One Step Forward

Take one little step forward. Don't worry about whether it's perfect, or what other people will think, or why you didn't do it sooner. Just take that one little step. And notice how good, how right it feels.

Take that one little step forward, and then take another. Suddenly, momentum is on your side. Yes, new and difficult challenges will surely arise, now that you're moving forward. As you climb higher, the terrain will likely become steeper and more rugged.

Yet whatever you're able to reach, you're also able to handle. With each step forward, you build the strength and the confidence to take the next step.

Right now is the time to take that next little steps forward, without hesitation, with no worries or complaints or regrets. And you'll quickly be so very thankful that you did.

Ralph Marston
The Daily Motivator
http://greatday.com

YOUR CROSS

Whatever your cross

Whatever your pain

There will always be sunshine

After the rain.

Perhaps you may stumble

Perhaps even fall

But God's always there

To help you through it all.

Author Unknown

For additional copies of this book or information concerning the author, visit our website at **www.ewestbooks.com** or send an email to the address below:

Email: eldererw@yahoo.com
Elder Elaine R. Westbrook
E. R. Westbrook Ministries
Memphis, TN

> "*You would be limping badly, spiritually, without the Holy Spirit. God gives us this fullness of the Spirit.*"
>
> *John MacArthur*
> *The Source of Spiritual Gifts*